The
Please Stop
Laughing at Me...
Journal

A Safe Place
for Us to Talk

Jodee Blanco

Author of the *New York Times* Bestseller
Please Stop Laughing at Me...

Avon, Massachusetts

Published by
Adams Media, a division of F+W Media, Inc.
57 Littlefield Street, Avon, MA 02322. U.S.A.
www.adamsmedia.com

Contains material adapted and abridged from *Please Stop Laughing at Me . . .* ,
by Jodee Blanco, copyright © 2010, 2003 by Jodee Blanco,
ISBN 10: 1-4405-0986-7, ISBN 13: 978-1-4405-0986-5.

ISBN 10: 1-4405-2809-8
ISBN 13: 978-1-4405-2809-5

Printed by RR Donnelley, Harrisonburg, VA, US
10   9   8   7   6   5   4   3   2   1
December 2011

This publication is designed to provide accurate and authoritative information
with regard to the subject matter covered. It is sold with the understanding that
the publisher is not engaged in rendering legal, accounting, or other professional
advice. If legal advice or other expert assistance is required, the services of a com-
petent professional person should be sought.

—From a *Declaration of Principles* jointly adopted by a Committee of the
American Bar Association and a Committee of Publishers and Associations

Many of the designations used by manufacturers and sellers to distinguish their
product are claimed as trademarks. Where those designations appear in this
book and Adams Media was aware of a trademark claim, the designations have
been printed with initial capital letters.

This book is available at quantity discounts for bulk purchases.
For information, please call 1-800-289-0963.

Contents

Introduction

Hello, it's good to meet you. My name is Jodee Blanco. From fifth grade through high school I was the school outcast for the same reason so many other kids today struggle to fit in, simply for being different. I was teased, taunted, kicked, spat on, and laughed at. And the harder I tried to make friends, the worse I was bullied. For me the worst part wasn't the abuse; it was the isolation, the ache to belong that seemed to go on forever inside me. You may have read my memoir *Please Stop Laughing at Me . . .* that chronicles what happened or its sequel *Please Stop Laughing at Us . . .*

I'm a successful adult now but I haven't forgotten those lonely years. In fact, I talk about them every day in schools all across the country, where I share my story with students, teachers, and parents to motivate change and awareness. My message is always threefold: It's not just joking around, bullying damages you for life; bullying isn't just the overt acts of cruelty, it's also the deliberate omission of compassion, that not being included is bullying too; and that if you are ostracized or picked on, there's nothing wrong with you. It's usually everything that's right about someone that makes them a target of abuse. Sometimes, after I've given a presentation, students will want to sit down with me and share their stories. I always take the time to listen, and afterwards, they often tell me how much better they feel having opened up to someone who understands what they're going through firsthand. And it's a moving experience for me to know that all the bullying I endured as a teen had a purpose, that it's enabling me to save lives today.

I wrote this journal so that you and I could get to know each other in much the same way I do with the students who approach me after they've heard me speak at their schools and want to talk.

Let me explain how I've structured this journal and how to achieve the most out of our time together.

It's divided into four sections. The first, Book One, entitled "Your Story," is a guided diary. It's broken down into themes inspired by select passages from *Please Stop Laughing at Me . . .* These are italicized. After each passage I include some questions as a writing prompt. Then, I give you really cool ideas and suggestions on everything from how to communicate more effectively with adults to the best way to handle a bully. The second section, Book Two, entitled "Your Poetry," lets you express yourself through writing poems, one of the most effective ways to release strong emotions. Book Three, which is called "Your Letters," gives you a chance to say the things you've wanted to say to different people in your life but haven't. And Book Four, entitled "Your Words to Your Future Self," is a place where you'll leave three messages for yourself to be read five, ten, and twenty years from now.

I wanted this journal to be more than the sum of its parts. I wanted it to be both a comfort and a means to deeper self-understanding, and a tool that you'll be able to use throughout your whole life. Promise me that you'll be open and honest in these pages, that you won't be afraid to tell the truth. I won't ever judge you or tell you how to feel. I'm here as your friend, confidante, and guide. Take my hand and let's begin.

book one

Your Story

The Bus

Swallowing hard, I navigate my way to a seat. The bus is crowded and, for a moment, I panic. The only seat available is at the very front, across from the driver. I bristle at the idea of starting my first day of high school in the "loser's seat." It's as if my fate is being sealed before I even step foot on school grounds. Clutching my book bag, I move gingerly toward the front of the bus. It's like walking the plank to social oblivion.

How do you get treated on the bus? What have some of your experiences been? Have you ever felt badly for someone else on the bus?

_____

_____

_____

_____

_____

_____

_____

_____

_____

_____

_____

_____

_____

_____

The next time you're on the bus and you start to feel frustrated or sad, get out your notebook and make a list of five new things you'd like to try before the end of the school year. They could be anything you want: an activity like community theater, dance, or joining a club, a cool sport you've never done before, a food you've always wanted to try. Then, when you get home, share the list with your parents and see if they can help you achieve the items on your wish list. This will give you something enjoyable to concentrate on during the bus ride.

I'd also like to give you some advice on how to deal with the bus bullies. Tell your parents what's going on. Give them the names of other kids on the bus who are being picked on too and encourage your mom and dad to contact their parents. Maybe your parents could start a car pool with them or they could approach the school together as a unit. That way you won't feel like it's just your family telling on the bullies. You're part of a group. It will also get the school to listen more seriously to any complaints.

Parents

My mom and dad raised me to come to them with any problems, and said that I should never be afraid to confide in them, regardless of the circumstances. They instilled in me a strong sense of right and wrong. They taught me to be compassionate and tolerant, and to reach out to the underdog. My mom and dad also encouraged me to act independently, and to have a mind of my own. It's served me well as a grown-up and now I'm grateful that they raised me to be my own person, but when I was in school, a lot of my classmates just thought I was weird.

What kind of relationship do you have with your parents, and do you feel like you can talk to them? What are some of your best moments with your parents? What are some of your most difficult experiences with them?

_____

_____

_____

_____

_____

_____

_____

_____

_____

_____

_____

Come up with five words that describe your relationship with your parents when everything is cool and you're getting along with them, and five words that describe what it's like when you're not. Then, make a collage based on those words. Cut out photos from magazines or newspapers, and let your imagination guide you. Next time you want to talk to your parents but don't know how to start the conversation, use the collage to help you.

Feeling Invisible

Many of my classmates had started forming cliques. Being accepted by one of these groups was all that mattered. You were either in or out. If you weren't a cheerleader or an athlete, an honor student or a member of the "cool" crowd, you might as well have been invisible.

Do you ever feel invisible at school?

_____

_____

_____

_____

_____

_____

_____

_____

_____

_____

_____

_____

_____

_____

Make a list of what you like most about yourself. Hang it up where you will see it every morning before school. Keep on adding to the list and when you run out of space on the paper, start a new list. Save these lists in a special place, and whenever you feel invisible, pull them out and read them.

Ignoring Bullies

My parents told me to ignore the bullies and walk away. They would never know how desperately wrong that advice was.

What advice have you been given about how to deal with the mean kids? Did you follow it? What happened?

_____

_____

_____

_____

_____

_____

_____

_____

_____

_____

_____

_____

_____

_____

_____

_____

Standing up for yourself nonviolently in the moment abuse occurs is your human right: Violence and vengeance are the wrongs. The next time someone bullies you, look that person in the eye, show no emotion, and tell him or her to stop. Even if it doesn't work, what matters most is that you stood up for yourself, a skill you will use your whole life. Start practicing it now.

Bullying by Omission

Bullying isn't just the mean things you do, it's all the nice things you never do: letting someone sit alone at lunch or excluding someone from a party even though you know that person would give almost anything to be invited.

In what ways do you feel overlooked by the kids at school? Is it possible you may have excluded someone without even being aware of it? What happened?

_____

_____

_____

_____

_____

_____

_____

_____

_____

_____

_____

_____

_____

_____

_____

Next time at lunch, go up to someone who's sitting alone or whom no one is talking to and ask if you could sit with him or her. Start a conversation about the bullying at your school and share some of your experiences. It could be the beginning of a lifelong friendship.

Hopes and Dreams

Dreams are but distant realities.

What does that statement mean to you? What are your hopes and dreams for the future?

_____

_____

_____

_____

_____

_____

_____

_____

_____

_____

_____

_____

_____

_____

_____

_____

_____

_____

Write down your biggest dream for your future. Then, every day, do one thing towards reaching that goal. For example, if your dream is to be a writer, you've already started by talking with me in this journal! If your dream is to be an actor, read a book about acting, watch a favorite movie, and pay attention to how the actors deliver their lines, or try out for a play. Each day you should be dedicating at least a few moments towards fulfilling your dream. Every action will bring you closer.

Conforming

The handicapped weren't the only targets. Anyone who chose to be different was picked on. It was either conform or be cast out. I couldn't do it.

Have you ever been bullied or excluded because you couldn't conform either? Did you ever try to conform even though it felt wrong? What happened and how did the experience affect you?

_____

_____

_____

_____

_____

_____

_____

_____

_____

_____

_____

_____

_____

_____

_____

_____

_____

Choose three favorite songs that speak to the deepest part of your heart. Put them on your iPod, and print out the lyrics and keep them with you. Whenever you feel as if no one understands you, listen to the songs or read the lyrics. The artists who wrote those songs felt just like you do. You're not as alone as you think.

Feeling Guilty

When I was the outcast, I never thought about the other kids who were also getting rejected. I couldn't see past my own pain. It never occurred to me that one day I would be the source of such pain.

Have you ever felt guilty about something you said or did to a classmate? Did you try to make it up to this person? How did things turn out?

_____

_____

_____

_____

_____

_____

_____

_____

_____

_____

_____

_____

_____

_____

Chances are you're not the only person at school who may be struggling to fit in. Pay attention to others in your class who are being bullied or excluded and reach out to them in friendship. Start tomorrow. Pick one person and ask if they'd like to hang out with you this weekend.

Physical Bullying

Kat would bump into me in the halls, shoving me into the lockers. Dara would kick me in the legs and shins. One afternoon in the lavatory, she tried to burn the inside of my wrist with a lit cigarette. I attempted to scream, but Jackie clamped her hand across my mouth, and told me if I made a sound, she and Dara would beat me until I bled.

Have you ever been physically abused by anyone? Do you know someone who has been?

_____

_____

_____

_____

_____

_____

_____

_____

_____

_____

_____

_____

_____

_____

_____

_____

No one has the right to hit or hurt another person. If you've ever been physically abused or know someone who has, write it down and then tell an adult you trust. Even if it happened a long time ago, tell someone right away.

Confiding in Someone

Lying on the pavement, curled up in a ball, listening to them laugh at me, all I could think of was how I was going to explain what happened to me when I arrived home. My jacket and pants were ripped and filthy. My hair was full of gravel and spit. My arms were scratched and bruised. Not knowing what else to do, I went to the nurse's office. "I was running to class and fell," I fibbed.

Have you ever felt so humiliated that you tried to hide what was happening? Has anyone ever confided in you about how they were being bullied? Who do you confide in?

_____

_____

_____

_____

_____

_____

_____

_____

_____

_____

_____

_____

_____

Tell your school counselor you have a suggestion to help bullied students. Encourage your counselor to place a drop box near the library where students can anonymously report incidents of bullying by writing them down and slipping the notes into the box. Then, be the first person to contribute a note. Taking action will make you feel empowered.

Feeling Like an Outsider in Your Own Life

My parents thought I was exaggerating what was happening at school. I knew there was nothing I could say or do to change my parents' minds. I had become an outsider in my own life. Who I believed I was no longer mattered. It was what my parents, teachers, classmates, and now doctors thought about me that counted. I was so tired of being a hostage to everyone else's opinions that I couldn't hear myself think anymore. My world had turned into a circus and I was the freak.

Have you ever felt this way? How did you handle it?

_____

_____

_____

_____

_____

_____

_____

_____

_____

_____

_____

_____

_____

_____

Think of a favorite movie or song that expresses some of the frustration you're feeling and share it with your parents. Afterwards, talk about it, and refer to the example of the movie or song to help your parents better understand where you're coming from. If you're using a song, make sure you print out the lyrics for your mom and dad so they can follow along as they listen to it.

Dark Thoughts

Whereas I used to close my eyes and envision being invited to parties and hanging out with the popular crowd, now I fantasized about hurting people. I didn't dare tell anyone.

Do you ever have dark thoughts? What are they? How do you cope? Are they getting worse or better?

_____

_____

_____

_____

_____

_____

_____

_____

_____

_____

_____

_____

_____

_____

_____

_____

First, you have to tell your parents or an adult you're comfortable talking to about these thoughts. Then, ask that adult to buy you a calendar. Every time you have a dark thought that won't go away, write it down, and then circle the day on the calendar that you had the thought. And if your parent or guardian wants you to see a therapist, I want you to do as they ask. Bring your notes and your calendar with you. And don't be afraid. I see a therapist sometimes when I'm really stressed out and it's good to be able to talk things out with an objective person who won't judge you.

A Special Place

Whenever one of us had a problem we'd all gather at the tree house to discuss it. The tree house was our escape from the adult world, a place where we could share our secrets without fear of judgment or punishment. We pondered the mysteries of sex and dating, talked about what we would be when we grew up, and vented the angst and frustrations of adolescence.

Do you and your friends have a special place together? What kinds of things do you talk about there? Is there a special place where you like to be alone to think?

_____

_____

_____

_____

_____

_____

_____

_____

_____

_____

_____

_____

_____

Any place can be a special place: your bedroom, a quiet spot in the backyard, a favorite park. Choose your own special place and write your next entry in this journal from there.

Home Life

I was one of the lucky ones. At least my parents had a good marriage. Some of the other kids at school weren't so fortunate.

What's your home life like? Are your parents married or divorced? How does your current home life affect you at school?

_____

_____

_____

_____

_____

_____

_____

_____

_____

_____

_____

_____

_____

_____

_____

_____

It's so easy to get caught up in our own problems and not notice when someone else is hurting and needs support. Next time you're with your family, notice everyone's demeanor. Does your mom seem sad or agitated? Is your dad more tired than usual? If one of your family members seems under the weather, offer a hug or a heartfelt compliment. Perform an unexpected act of kindness for that person. It will make you feel better too!

Being Yourself

The truth stank. It was either be liked by everyone but hate yourself, or respect yourself and be hated by everyone. What a choice. I didn't know how much longer I could keep up this charade. Teenagers are perceptive. Eventually, my classmates would figure out that my "coolness" was an act. I was so tired of pretending to be someone I wasn't just to ensure my social status at school. Soon, my resolve weakened.

Have you ever pretended to be someone you're not to gain the acceptance of others? If so, how did it make you feel? If not, what helped you stay strong?

_____

_____

_____

_____

_____

_____

_____

_____

_____

_____

_____

_____

Do you have a friend who seems to have completely changed? Maybe he or she turned on you without reason or warning. Perhaps he or she started hanging out with new people and stopped spending time with you. I'd like you to tell this person how they made you feel, not in a mean, angry way, but with kindness. You can do it in a letter or e-mail if you prefer. The purpose of this exercise is to help you become more comfortable communicating openly to someone when they've hurt you. And maybe, your friend will come around. Sometimes all that stands in the way of fixing a friendship is that neither person wants to be the first to try and talk things out. Take the leap. And don't worry about whether or not things end the way you'd like them to. What's important is that you learned you have the courage to face the people you care about and tell them how you feel. I'm very proud of you!

Bystanders and Rescuers

After the attack at the bus stop, I kept to myself more than ever at school.
Emily and Kim both felt guilty about what had happened and tried to
make things right. "After all, the boys were the ones who threw the rocks
at you, not us. We didn't do anything."

"That's exactly the point," I said. "You both stood there and watched
and didn't do a thing to help me. You could have at least told them to
stop."

"We said we're sorry," Kim retorted.

"It's just that nobody likes you anymore, and if we stick up for you,
the same could happen to us," Emily explained. "It's nothing personal.
We still think you're okay."

They honestly didn't believe they were at fault. If the situation were
reversed, I would have tried to stop those boys or I would have found an
adult to help. They did nothing. To me, that made them worse.

What's the worst experience you ever had with bystanders? Has
anyone ever stood up for you? Have you ever been a bystander? A
rescuer? If you could say anything to the bystanders at your school,
what would you tell them?

_____

_____

_____

_____

_____

_____

_____

The next time you see someone getting picked on at school, I want you to try this rescue method. You can also teach it to your friends and ask them to use it if you're being bullied. It's called "The Diversion." Let's say you have a classmate named Susie and a group of mean kids is harassing her. Create any excuse (the simpler the better) that will enable you to whisk her away. For example, try shouting out, "Susie, my locker's stuck. Could you help me?" Or, "Susie, there's a phone call for you in the main office." Then, grab her hand and lead her out of harm's way.

Popularity

There are two types of popular kids in school: "Elite Leaders™" are the members of the cool crowd who are kind and inclusive; "Elite Tormentors™" are the mean popular kids who use exclusion like a weapon.

Who are the Elite Tormentors™ in your school? Who are the Elite Leaders™?

_____

_____

_____

_____

_____

_____

_____

_____

_____

_____

_____

_____

_____

_____

_____

_____

If an Elite Tormentor™ is bullying you, reach out to one of the Elite Leaders™ and ask for help and support. Most Elite Leaders™ want to help but they may not know you're in trouble unless you tell them.

The Irony

I hated myself. It was my strength that made my classmates pick on me in the first place, but it was my weakness that allowed their viciousness to flourish. What a mess.

What does this statement mean to you? Do you have certain personal strengths that your classmates make fun of; and in what ways, if any, do you allow them to put you down? What would you like to change about the entire situation if you could?

_____

_____

_____

_____

_____

_____

_____

_____

_____

_____

_____

_____

_____

_____

_____

Now that you've gotten that off your chest, go do something physical. Go for a bike ride or a brisk walk. Shoot some hoops. If you're not able to exercise because of an injury or condition, do something fun that you enjoy. Sometimes the best way to harness your inner strength is to tap into your physical energy.

Feeling Powerless

It seemed as if everyone had power over my life except me: my parents, my teachers, my school principal, even the bullies.

Do you ever feel this way? If you could say anything to the people in your life who make you feel powerless, what would you like to tell them and why?

_____

_____

_____

_____

_____

_____

_____

_____

_____

_____

_____

_____

_____

_____

_____

_____

If you want to feel more in control, it starts with learning how to communicate effectively with adults. Sit down with your parents or an adult you trust and be honest about what's upsetting you and why. Here are some suggested conversation starters. All you have to do is fill in the blanks. "I feel _____ because _____." "It would help me a lot if _____." "In return, I'm willing to _____." And remember to be kind and patient. Don't have an attitude. Listen to whatever the adult has to say and if you don't agree with something, respond truthfully but with respect.

The Hallways

Every day when the bell rang at the end of each period, I froze with fear. Walking the halls had become an exercise in terror. "You better get a bodyguard, because we're going to beat you senseless," A.J. whispered in my ear one morning outside math class. After that, I didn't dare look anyone in the eye when I passed through the halls between classes because seeing their fury was too scary.

What are the hallways like for you at school? Are there certain people who always seem to get picked on in between periods? Are you one of them?

_____

_____

_____

_____

_____

_____

_____

_____

_____

_____

_____

_____

Keep your eyes peeled the next time you're walking to class. Make a mental list of who seems to get bullied the most. Maybe it's you or perhaps it's someone else. Then make a decision to do something about it. Submit a written report (you don't have to sign your name if you don't want to—you can sign it "a concerned student") to the principal that lists who gets bullied when, and request that he ask the faculty to keep closer watch during period changes.

Phony Friends

What a desperate, pathetic fool I was. Time after time, my "friends" had shown me their true colors. Yet, I still wanted to believe they were sorry for causing me pain. I was becoming just like the character of the battered wife in those cheesy made-for-TV movies about domestic violence. No matter how often I got abused or degraded, I kept going back for more, convincing myself that things would change, and if they didn't, it was my fault. What was wrong with me?

Do you have any phony friends who you keep allowing to hurt you? What are the qualities of a true friend? Tell me about your best friend.

_____

_____

_____

_____

_____

_____

_____

_____

_____

_____

_____

_____

If you're struggling to figure out which of your friends are true, and which are phony, make a list for each friend, and make two columns. Label one column "what I like and respect most about this person," and label the other, "what I don't like about this person." If the second column is significantly longer than the first, you may want to rethink the friendship.

The Price of Popularity

Cruelty is currency in high school. It can buy power and popularity.

Has anyone ever tried to look cool in front of his or her friends by being mean to you or someone else? Have you ever tried to win a friendship at someone else's expense? How did the experience make you feel?

_____

_____

_____

_____

_____

_____

_____

_____

_____

_____

_____

_____

_____

_____

_____

_____

_____

_____

Start a scrapbook that reveals what you're feeling and experiencing during this period of your life. Be as creative and imaginative as you like. When something meaningful happens, good or bad, dedicate a page to it. Use the scrapbook as a means to visually express what's going on inside of you and around you.

Finding Yourself

The hardest thing about being the outcast isn't the love you don't receive. It's the love you long to give that nobody wants. After a while, it backs up into your system like stagnant water and turns toxic, poisoning your spirit. When this happens, you don't have many choices available. You can become a bitter loner who goes through life being pissed off at the world; you can fester with rage. Or you can find another outlet for your love, where it will be appreciated and maybe even returned.

Do you sometimes feel like, no matter how hard you try, you don't fit in?

_____

_____

_____

_____

_____

_____

_____

_____

_____

_____

_____

_____

_____

Be a volunteer. Ask your parents or a teacher if there's some-place where you could give your time to make a difference in the lives of others—an animal shelter, a hospital, your local park district. The key is to find volunteer work or community service that makes you feel valued and appreciated by those you help. Not only is it emotionally rewarding, it's also good for your resume.

Real Friends

Would I like to be part of the popular crowd? Yes, desperately. Do I long to go on dates and be invited to all the cool parties? More than words can say. But maybe those things aren't so important. Maybe I should embrace the love right in front of me.

Do you ever find yourself trying so hard to make certain kids like you that you lose sight of the amazing friends you already have? How do you show the people in your life who are there for you that you appreciate them?

_____

_____

_____

_____

_____

_____

_____

_____

_____

_____

_____

_____

_____

_____

On the days that school feels extra awful and the mean kids are really getting to you, focus on the friends you do have, even if it's just one person. Make plans to hang out together on the weekend. Join an activity at the park district together. The more you appreciate those who like you for who you are, the stronger you'll be when dealing with the bullies.

Being Laughed At

I know they're talking about me. I can tell by the looks on their faces. Then they burst into laughter. How I hate that sound. It's gotten to the point that when my parents invite people over and I hear them laughing over a conversation at dinner, it makes me cringe.

Do your classmates laugh at you? Have you ever laughed at someone? Tell me what happened.

_____

_____

_____

_____

_____

_____

_____

_____

_____

_____

_____

_____

_____

Ask your counselor or principal if you can start an anti-bullying campaign at your school in the form of a poster contest. Form a committee and invite fellow classmates who are also being laughed at and picked on to join. Make sure the school assigns a faculty member to supervise. And remember, taking action by motivating action in others is how the world is changed, one determined heart at a time.

Teachers

English class is kind of a drag. The instructor, Mr. Jobes, cares more about being liked by his students than about being respected by them. He rarely disciplines anyone. His daughter Lisa, a high-ranking member of the in-crowd, delights in showing off her superiority. Nothing gives her more pleasure than to test the power of her popularity by instigating verbal attacks against someone, and seeing how many others she can persuade to join in.

Tell me about your teachers. Who do you feel comfortable talking to and why? Who's given you support when you've needed it? And how have some teachers disappointed you?

_____

_____

_____

_____

_____

_____

_____

_____

_____

_____

_____

_____

Write your favorite teacher a thank-you note expressing the reasons why you appreciate his or her presence in your life. And if you're having trouble with another teacher, ask your favorite teacher to help you figure out how best to approach the problem. And remember to always be respectful and kind.

Peer Pressure

Mark, Nadia, Shelly, and several others from their clique are in my class. I've managed to hold my own with them by exercising self-discipline. Even when I'm itching to participate in class because it's a topic of particular interest to me, I keep my mouth shut. So far, it's working. Nobody is calling me "teacher's pet" behind my back during class. I probably won't get as good of a grade as I could have if I raised my hand more often, but not being the butt of everyone's jokes is well worth the tradeoff.

Have you ever done something that wasn't good for you because you were afraid you'd be excluded or made fun of if you didn't? How did it make you feel? What was the result? What did you learn about yourself from this experience?

_____

_____

_____

_____

_____

_____

_____

_____

_____

_____

_____

_____

Keep a small notepad with you. Every time you give in to peer pressure, whether someone pushes you into it or it's your own fear of what others will think that makes you do it, put a check mark in the notebook. At the end of each week, count how many checkmarks you have. Each week that you have fewer checkmarks than the week before, congratulate yourself and know that I'm proud of you.

Being Different

Being different can be a social death warrant when you're fourteen. I didn't choose to be different any more than someone chooses to be gay or tall. You don't get to pick who you are in this life, but you can decide what you become.

Do you ever feel different? What would you want to change about yourself if you could? What would you never want to change? How do you see the future adult version of you? What will he or she be like?

_____

_____

_____

_____

_____

_____

_____

_____

_____

_____

_____

_____

_____

_____

Make a wish list of questions you'd like to know the answers to by the time you're an adult and fold the list and keep it inside this journal. Pull out the list periodically, and as the answers reveal themselves to you, put a checkmark next to those questions. If you're living life to the fullest, you'll always be adding questions and checkmarks to your list. When or if you become a parent, share this list with your children. You'll know when they're ready.

Afraid to Say "No"

Some of the meanest kids in school are probably compassionate and sensitive on the inside, but they think that to be accepted, they have to be willing to be cruel once in a while. Most of them will do almost anything to avoid being alone.

What's the worst thing anyone ever asked you to do? Did you do it? Why or why not? Tell me the story.

_____

_____

_____

_____

_____

_____

_____

_____

_____

_____

_____

_____

_____

_____

_____

_____

Practice saying "no" with confidence when someone wants you to do something that doesn't feel right to you. Start today. And let me know what happens. Jot it down on a piece of paper if you don't have your journal with you. I'm rooting for you.

Self-Loathing

I hate who I am. I don't want to be this person anymore. When I look in the mirror, I loathe who I see.

Do you ever feel this way? Why? Have you talked to anyone about it?

_____

_____

_____

_____

_____

_____

_____

_____

_____

_____

_____

_____

_____

_____

_____

_____

The next time you look in the mirror, I want you to say these words out loud, "I am strong. I am beautiful. I am brave. I am (insert your name here) and I will make my mark in this world. No one and nothing can stop me from becoming all that I'm meant to be." That's called an affirmation. I'd like you to create some of your own affirmations. Ask friends and family members who know you well to help you. Your affirmations can be as funny and personal as you like, but nothing negative, only positive things about you. Write them on index cards and when you start to feel down about yourself, pull out one of the cards, stand in front of the mirror, and read your affirmation. And yes, it's okay if sometimes it makes you giggle.

Being the Victim

The bully never remembers, the victim never forgets.

Has that ever happened to you? Were you the bully, the victim, or the bystander? Do you think bystanders forget too? What did you learn from the experience?

_____

_____

_____

_____

_____

_____

_____

_____

_____

_____

_____

_____

_____

_____

_____

_____

Pretend that it's twenty years from now and the night of your school reunion. If you could say anything to the bullies, what would it be? Write it down on a piece of paper and tuck it away in this journal. One day you may use it. You'll know if you're ready.

The Loneliness

It's Friday night. The weekend spreads out before me like a vast waste-land. I close my eyes to try and shut out the loneliness. I feel like I'm losing my mind.

When have you felt the loneliest? Why?

_____

_____

_____

_____

_____

_____

_____

_____

_____

_____

_____

_____

_____

_____

_____

_____

There's a great big world waiting for you and new friends that you simply haven't met yet. Find a social outlet separate from school. Visit the websites of the largest park district and local public library two to three towns away from your community and look up their organized activities for teens. Most offer everything from youth theater, dance, and soccer, to book clubs, cheerleading, and craft clubs. Choose an activity you'd like to try and ask your parents to enroll you. But it's important it be located far enough away that you'll make new friends with new faces. It will give you something to look forward to and help you feel less alone.

Avoiding School

When my alarm goes off, I hide under the covers, fold my hands, and pray that I am suddenly stricken with mono or strep throat—anything contagious that will prevent me from going to school.

Have you ever faked being sick or made yourself sick to avoid school? Do you know someone who has? What happened?

_____

_____

_____

_____

_____

_____

_____

_____

_____

_____

_____

_____

_____

_____

_____

_____

If your situation has gotten bad enough that you'll do almost anything to get out of going to school, you need to take action right now. Tell your parents or an adult you trust that you need support. If it's easier, write it in an e-mail or a letter. But you need to speak up and ask for help. Do not put it off any longer. If you've already reached out for help and things are not any better, talk to someone else, a teacher, a counselor, the parent of a friend. Don't give up. Never, ever give up.

Secret Envy

I watch couples kissing in the school yard or in the halls and the cheer-leaders in their short skirts and tight sweaters smiling and laughing, shar-ing secrets, exchanging makeup. What I wouldn't give for just one day of what they have.

Do you ever envy some of your classmates? What is it that you envy most? Why? Do you think any of them are jealous of you? If so, who?

_____

_____

_____

_____

_____

_____

_____

_____

_____

_____

_____

_____

_____

_____

_____

_____

It's natural to experience envy sometimes. The next time you find yourself daydreaming about trading places with one of your classmates, ask a mutual friend about that person's life. You may discover he or she doesn't have it as perfect as you thought. Then, reach out a hand in friendship. You may be surprised by the results.

You Just Don't Understand

Why must Mom continue pushing her grown-up logic on me? Kids simply don't think that way. Adults perceive the act of ignoring someone as a sign of power. Teenagers think it spells weakness with a capital "W." The more I pretend indifference, the harder my classmates try to get my goat. Mom just doesn't get it: Teens are different than adults. I care about my mom's opinion of me, and it's really causing a predicament. Instead of fighting back at school, which is what I should do, I try to act mature and walk away because I don't want my mom to be disappointed in me. But what about my own sense of self? Mom is so worried about my dignity that she never stops to consider my pride.

What's the most effective advice you've been given by an adult? What's the worst advice you've gotten and why don't you think it worked?

_____

_____

_____

_____

_____

_____

_____

_____

_____

_____

Kids learn from adults, but adults can also learn a lot from kids. Sit down with an adult who's given you good advice, thank them, and explain why their advice helped you. Let them know how grateful you are. And if there's someone whose suggestions didn't work out too well, thank that person for the support, but with kindness and respect, explain how the situation turned out. It's okay to be honest. Sometimes if we're not, resentment can build, and no one, especially when all they did was try to help, deserves our resentment. The more you practice communicating openly, the more those you care about most will understand you.

Telling on Someone

I can't run because they have me surrounded. If I scream and get a teacher's attention I could get them into trouble. I have to make a choice. I either let them degrade me now and get it over with, or attempt rescue from a teacher and be tortured later for being a snitch. "Come on you guys, please let me go to class," I plead. For a brief moment, I see guilt flicker across several faces, but I know no one will risk going against the pack. They encircle me.

Have you ever wanted to ask for help but were afraid everyone at school would label you a tattletale or a snitch if you did? What did you end up doing? What happened?

_____

_____

_____

_____

_____

_____

_____

_____

_____

_____

_____

In most cases, bullying is a cry for help. Often the bully needs love and support as much or more than the victim. There's a difference between tattling and telling. Tattling is when you report something only because you want to get the bully into trouble and that's not cool. Telling is different. That's when you report a bullying incident because you have concern for everyone involved. Tattling is an act of betrayal. Telling is the ultimate act of courage and compassion. Next time you or someone you know is being bullied, report it. You could be saving the life of the bully too.

Pretending Everything Is Fine When It's Not

When I get home from school, my parents ask me if anything is wrong. I can't bear for them to start worrying about me again. I lie and tell them everything is fine.

Have you ever lied to your parents? What did you lie about and why? Did you ever end up telling them the truth? What happened?

_____

_____

_____

_____

_____

_____

_____

_____

_____

_____

_____

_____

_____

_____

_____

_____

Lying and pretending only makes things worse. If you're uncomfortable or afraid to tell your parents what's going on, put it in a letter and give it to them. Or if you like, you could pick out some passages from this journal to read out loud to them. Another option, talk to your school counselor or a favorite teacher and ask if they'd speak to your parents with you. No matter what, tell someone the truth. Ask for help. No more being silent.

The Lunchroom

Since the incident after gym, my classmates have decided they won't allow a "freak" like me to eat in their lunchroom. When they see me at the soda machines, they threaten to beat me. They have made me so scared that I start stuffing my book bag with protein bars each morning before school. Then, at lunchtime, I sneak into the girls' bathroom, sit on the sink, and wolf them down. I have nowhere else to go.

What's your lunchroom experience like at school? Do you have someone to sit with? Do you notice any classmates who sit alone every day?

_____

_____

_____

_____

_____

_____

_____

_____

_____

_____

_____

_____

_____

Like we talked about earlier, reach out to someone who's sitting alone and ask to sit with him or her. Start a conversation about the bullying at your school. Try to make a friend. If that doesn't work, talk to your principal or counselor about the possibility of using your lunch period to study at the library or help out in the nurse's office. Just make sure you have a healthy snack and that you don't go all day without eating.

Wanting Out

I wish the universe would rush the passage of time so that years would turn into months, and days would become hours. I realize it's probably a sin to think like this, but I want my teen years to finish. If they don't end soon, I fear they may finish me.

Do you ever feel this way? Do you have any moments that you wished didn't go by so fast, that were so special you wished they would have lasted forever?

_____

_____

_____

_____

_____

_____

_____

_____

_____

_____

_____

_____

_____

_____

The next time you experience something really wonderful, drink in every detail. Let your memory absorb the sounds, smells, colors, and sensations. When you're going through a difficult time, close your eyes and relive that good moment; let it fill you up inside. Then, take a deep breath, open your eyes, and remind yourself that you're strong and smart and can get through this.

Personal Angels

I've been blessed. Despite getting knocked down so many times, God keeps putting people in my corner at just the right time who give me the courage and strength to come out for one more round. Often, the opponent isn't another fighter, but my own self-doubt.

Who are the people in your life who give you courage and confidence?

_____

_____

_____

_____

_____

_____

_____

_____

_____

_____

_____

_____

_____

_____

_____

_____

Make a list of your most ardent supporters. Then, come up with a gift idea for each of them—nothing material, a gesture from your heart. It could be an act of kindness, a handwritten thank-you note, an art or craft project that you make, anything that lets them know how much you appreciate their presence in your life.

Celebrity Role Models

Some of the country's most successful people—musicians and moguls, authors and actors—were teen misfits, too. The heartache they endured at school defined their character and determination. Perhaps if they had it easy, they wouldn't have become who they are today.

Who are your favorite celebrities? What are the qualities you admire most about them?

_____

_____

_____

_____

_____

_____

_____

_____

_____

_____

_____

_____

_____

_____

_____

_____

Research your favorite celebrities. See if you can find out if they struggled to fit in when they were in school, or if they were bullied. Then write them a letter and share some of your experiences. Celebrities enjoy receiving fan mail, and while they may not be able to get to every letter, they do read as many of them as they can. Who knows? Yours may be one of the letters that reaches them personally.

Turning Pain Into Purpose

When you're a victim of any kind of abuse, you can do one of two things. You can learn how to turn your pain into purpose and make a difference in the world, or you can allow it to extinguish the light inside you.

What's the most painful experience you've ever had? How did you survive it? What advice do you have for someone else going through something similar?

_____

_____

_____

_____

_____

_____

_____

_____

_____

_____

_____

_____

_____

_____

_____

If you know someone who's going through a painful experience that you've gone through too, reach out and help that person. Offer support and advice. You could even take it a step further. For example, if you're being bullied at school, ask your counselor if you could start a support group for bullied students. Not only would you be transforming something negative in your life into something positive, but you'd be helping yourself and others. How amazing is that! Or maybe your parents are divorced and you start a support group at school for other students in the same situation. The bottom line is that if you can take difficult experiences from your own life and find a way to use them to empower others, it can help you to heal.

Trust

The first few weeks of senior year pass swiftly. Surprisingly, no one is giving me a hard time. I should be happy and relieved, but instead, it makes me suspicious. At least when I was getting teased and taunted, I knew what to expect.

Have you ever felt this way? Is it difficult for you to trust people or are you sometimes too trusting?

_____

_____

_____

_____

_____

_____

_____

_____

_____

_____

_____

_____

_____

_____

_____

If you're struggling with whether to trust a classmate or not, have your parents help you create a list of ten questions to ask yourself about your relationship with this person. Use the answers to help you make your decision.

Insecurity

I worry that when I'm older, I'll be so afraid that people won't like me that I'll have trouble believing it when they actually do.

When do you feel at your most insecure? How do you deal with it?

_____

_____

_____

_____

_____

_____

_____

_____

_____

_____

_____

_____

_____

_____

_____

_____

_____

Everyone has moments of insecurity. The trick is to have enough confidence to get past them. Engage in activities that you enjoy and that make you feel good about yourself. The more you reach out and live life to the fullest, the less insecure you'll be.

Making a Difference

I don't think the major events in a person's life are ever the result of chance. Things happen for a reason. I know that being rejected and hurt had a purpose in my life. Now I'm excited about learning what that purpose is.

What do you think your destiny is, your reason for being here on this earth? If you could change the world, what would you do and why?

_____

_____

_____

_____

_____

_____

_____

_____

_____

_____

_____

_____

_____

_____

_____

You can make a difference. All it takes is passion and purpose. Take an issue you care deeply about and research it. Then, ask one of your parents or a teacher to help you write a letter to your senator or congressman about this issue, why it's important to you personally, and why you think action must be taken. The results may surprise you.

Letting Go

I take a long, deep breath and do something I never thought I'd have the courage to do—but I know that I must in order to be free. I let go of all the hurt and anger that has held me secretly hostage all these years—the rage over tears shed and words never spoken. I let go of the bitterness and sadness, the loneliness that has haunted me, and the stale, unfulfilled daydreams of my youth.

Do you think you'll be able to let go of the bullying you've endured? How would you start? What would have to happen in order for you to move past the anger and find closure?

_____

_____

_____

_____

_____

_____

_____

_____

_____

_____

_____

_____

_____

_____

Make a list of everything you've ever wanted to say to the bullies but didn't. Get out all your anger on paper. Attach the list to a helium balloon and ask your friends and family to join you as you release the balloon into the air. Then celebrate your future with a renewed heart.

Your School Reunion

I slowly open my eyes and smile at my former classmates sitting before me. I can finally forgive them . . . and myself.

Years from now when you receive the invitation to your first school reunion what do you think your initial reaction will be? Do you think you'll go or are you more likely to avoid it? Why?

_____

_____

_____

_____

_____

_____

_____

_____

_____

_____

_____

_____

_____

_____

_____

_____

I know it may be hard, but I'd like to think you'll walk through those doors proud of who you are with no expectations other than how you're going to reward yourself the next day for your remarkable courage. It's also a good idea to attend with a loving, supportive friend who understands your insecurities and can be there to hold your hand when you need it. What happens at the reunion doesn't really matter. What's important is that you faced your fears and conquered them.

book two

Your Poetry

Finding the Poet
Inside You

I discovered solace in composing poems. The language of poetry gave me a way to transform my hurt and wrath into symbols and images that I could control. When my classmates snickered at me or whispered unkind names behind my back in study hall, I closed myself off from them by writing a poem and immersing myself in the soothing sound of the pen darting across the page.

Have you ever written a poem?

Here's one of the poems I composed when I was a teen. Hopefully it will help to get you started. And as you'll see, I certainly didn't hold anything back.

Revenge

You all think you're cool, stabbing my heart—
Bloodsucking vultures, ripping my life apart—
Thought you'd take a loser, feed on her pain—
But you're gonna pay—
I'm not running again,
Revenge—how sweet is the word.
Revenge—seems so absurd,
But justice will find you
She's just biding time
So suffer and bleed
Pay for your crime
Victims are running—
Frightened and blind—
Lost in a world that's sadly unkind—
The vicious and cruel have fed on their souls—
Left them shells—
Empty and cold—
Their eyes are full of hate—
They've vowed to get vengeance—
To defy their fate.

I'd like you to try writing a poem. It doesn't have to rhyme or follow any format or structure. Just let your feelings unleash themselves onto the paper. Don't second-guess yourself. Just pour out the contents of your heart. Let everything out: rage, anger, sadness, joy, fear, uncertainty, frustration, sadness, hope; whatever is there, set it free through your poetry. Don't think. Write.

book three

Your Letters

The Power of the Pen

Writing a letter to express your feelings can be a healing experience. I have a whole box of letters that I wrote and never ended up giving to the intended recipients. I didn't need to. The simple act of getting all those emotions off my chest made me feel better.

I'd like you to make a list of five people that you've wanted to talk to about something important but haven't. Maybe you were afraid or perhaps you didn't know where to begin. Maybe it's one of your parents, a friend, a teacher, a sibling, or a significant other. It might even be the bully who hurt you the most and you want him or her to know how you feel. Whoever it is, whatever the circumstance, use this opportunity to get everything off your chest in a letter. As with the poetry, don't hold back. Let it all out.

Letter to Person One

_____

_____

_____

_____

_____

_____

_____

_____

_____

_____

_____

_____

_____

_____

_____

_____

_____

_____

_____

_____

_____

Letter to Person Two

_____

_____

_____

_____

_____

_____

_____

_____

_____

_____

_____

_____

_____

_____

_____

_____

_____

_____

_____

_____

_____

_____

_____

_____

_____

Letter to Person Three

Letter to Person Four

_____

_____

_____

_____

_____

_____

_____

_____

_____

_____

_____

_____

_____

_____

_____

_____

_____

_____

_____

_____

_____

_____

_____

_____

Letter to Person Five

_____

_____

_____

_____

_____

_____

_____

_____

_____

_____

_____

_____

_____

_____

_____

_____

_____

_____

_____

_____

_____

_____

Reread each of your letters. If there are any you'd like to send, instead of pulling the page out of the journal, recopy the letter onto another piece of paper. Read it again; then wait at least one month before sending it. That way, you'll have a chance to make changes if you want to. You may also discover that unburdening yourself on paper was enough and that you don't need to send it. I support whatever you decide.

book four

*Your Words
to Your
Future Self*

Time Capsules

As you mature, your ideas and attitudes will evolve. The way you feel now about certain things in your life won't be how you feel five, ten, or twenty years from now. One of the advantages of growing older is that you gain a better understanding of who you are and what you want. One of the disadvantages is that sometimes life with all its ups and downs can make you forget about your dreams or lose sight of what once used to mean so much to you. I wish I would have written letters to myself when I was a teenager, reminding me of what was important to me then so I wouldn't ever lose sight of it now. To conclude our time together, I'd like you to write three letters to yourself: one for you to be opened five years from now, one for you to be opened ten years from today, and the last to be read twenty years from now. In these letters I want you to tell yourself what you care about most, what your dreams are for your future, the mistakes you want to avoid, all that you want to accomplish, what you look for in a spouse, if you dream about having children and how you envision them, what you've sworn you will do in your life no matter what, what you've promised yourself you'll never do—anything and everything you want your future self to know about you right now.

And don't forget to read each one when it's time.

Some Parting Thoughts Before You Go

Use this journal as a guide and a benchmark throughout your life. One day you may even wish to share some of its contents with your children. These pages contain the sacred truth of your heart, the bits and pieces of what makes you uniquely you.

I am deeply honored to have spent this meaningful time with you.

If you'd like to continue the conversation, please visit me at my website at *www.jodeeblanco.com*.

Until we talk again . . .